50 Brunch Bonanza Recipes for Home

By: Kelly Johnson

Table of Contents

- Classic Eggs Benedict
- Pancake Stack with Maple Syrup
- Smoked Salmon and Cream Cheese Croissants
- Spinach and Mushroom Quiche
- Cheddar and Chive Biscuits with Sausage Gravy
- Blueberry Almond French Toast Casserole
- Breakfast Tostadas with Avocado and Fried Eggs
- Coconut Mango Smoothie Bowl
- Ham and Cheese Breakfast Burritos
- Cinnamon Swirl Coffee Cake
- Caprese Breakfast Sandwich
- Quinoa and Veggie Breakfast Bowl
- Chocolate Hazelnut Stuffed Croissants
- Greek Yogurt and Berry Parfait
- Southwest Frittata with Black Beans and Corn
- Banana Walnut Pancakes
- Bacon and Hash Brown Breakfast Skillet
- Avocado and Tomato Breakfast Tacos
- Lemon Blueberry Muffins
- Breakfast Pizza with Eggs and Bacon
- Green Shakshuka with Spinach and Feta
- Raspberry Cheesecake Stuffed French Toast
- Veggie and Goat Cheese Omelette
- Apple Cider Donuts
- Chia Seed Pudding Parfait with Kiwi
- Sausage and Pepper Breakfast Burrito
- Peanut Butter Banana Pancakes
- Tomato Basil Bruschetta with Poached Eggs
- Strawberry Shortcake Waffles
- Mediterranean Quinoa Salad with Poached Eggs
- Breakfast BLT Wrap

- Pumpkin Spice Muffins
- Bacon and Egg Breakfast Quesadilla
- Berry Protein Smoothie Bowl
- Asparagus and Swiss Cheese Strata
- Cranberry Orange Scones
- Banana Chocolate Chip Waffles
- Bagel with Lox and Cream Cheese
- Sun-Dried Tomato and Basil Egg Muffins
- Blueberry Lemon Poppy Seed Pancakes
- Avocado and Bacon Breakfast Sandwich
- Pesto and Sundried Tomato Frittata
- Chocolate Banana Bread
- Cheesy Spinach and Artichoke Breakfast Casserole
- Vanilla Berry Parfait with Granola
- Ham and Swiss Croissant Sandwiches
- Sourdough Breakfast Strata with Ham and Gruyere
- Coconut Pineapple Smoothie Bowl
- Almond Joy Overnight Oats
- Breakfast Tiramisu French Toast

Classic Eggs Benedict

Ingredients:

    English muffins (split and toasted)
    Canadian bacon or ham (thinly sliced)
    Poached eggs
    Hollandaise sauce
    Fresh chives or parsley for garnish (optional)

Instructions:

Prepare the Hollandaise Sauce:
- Ingredients for Hollandaise sauce:
    - 3 egg yolks
    - 1 tablespoon lemon juice
    - 1/2 cup unsalted butter (melted)
    - Salt and cayenne pepper to taste
- Instructions:
    - In a blender or food processor, combine the egg yolks and lemon juice. Blend until smooth.
    - With the blender or food processor running, slowly drizzle in the melted butter until the sauce thickens.
    - Season with salt and a pinch of cayenne pepper. Blend again and set aside.

Poach the Eggs:
- Bring a pot of water to a gentle simmer.
- Crack each egg into a small bowl.
- Create a gentle whirlpool in the simmering water and carefully slide the egg into the center of the whirlpool.
- Poach each egg for about 3-4 minutes for a soft, runny yolk.

Assemble the Eggs Benedict:
- Toast the English muffin halves and place them on a plate.
- Top each English muffin half with a slice of Canadian bacon or ham.
- Carefully place a poached egg on top of each bacon-covered muffin half.

Drizzle with Hollandaise Sauce:
- Spoon a generous amount of Hollandaise sauce over each poached egg.

Garnish:

- Optionally, garnish the Eggs Benedict with fresh chopped chives or parsley.

Serve immediately while the eggs and sauce are still warm. This classic dish is known for its rich and creamy Hollandaise sauce complementing the perfectly poached eggs and savory Canadian bacon.

Pancake Stack with Maple Syrup

Ingredients:

    2 cups all-purpose flour
    2 tablespoons granulated sugar
    1 tablespoon baking powder
    1/2 teaspoon salt
    2 large eggs
    1 1/2 cups milk
    1/4 cup unsalted butter, melted
    1 teaspoon vanilla extract
    Maple syrup for serving
    Optional toppings: Fresh berries, sliced bananas, whipped cream

Instructions:

Mix Dry Ingredients:
- In a large mixing bowl, whisk together the flour, sugar, baking powder, and salt.

Prepare Wet Ingredients:
- In a separate bowl, beat the eggs and then add the milk, melted butter, and vanilla extract. Mix well.

Combine Wet and Dry Ingredients:
- Pour the wet ingredients into the dry ingredients and stir until just combined. Be careful not to overmix; a few lumps are okay.

Heat the Griddle or Pan:
- Preheat a griddle or non-stick skillet over medium heat. Lightly grease with butter or cooking spray.

Cook the Pancakes:
- Pour 1/4 cup of batter onto the griddle for each pancake. Cook until bubbles form on the surface, then flip and cook the other side until golden brown.

Stack the Pancakes:
- As each pancake is cooked, transfer it to a plate. Continue until you have a stack of delicious pancakes.

Serve with Maple Syrup:
- Pour warm maple syrup over the pancake stack. Use as much or as little as you prefer.

Optional Toppings:
- Garnish the pancake stack with fresh berries, sliced bananas, or a dollop of whipped cream for added flavor and presentation.

Enjoy:
- Serve the pancake stack immediately while they are warm. The fluffy texture and sweet maple syrup make this a delightful and classic breakfast treat.

Feel free to customize this basic pancake recipe with your favorite toppings and enjoy a comforting and delicious breakfast or brunch.

Smoked Salmon and Cream Cheese Croissants

Ingredients:

- 4 large croissants
- 8 ounces smoked salmon
- 1/2 cup cream cheese, softened
- 1 tablespoon fresh dill, chopped
- 1 tablespoon capers, drained
- 1 tablespoon red onion, finely chopped
- Lemon wedges for serving
- Freshly ground black pepper (optional)

Instructions:

Prepare the Croissants:
- Preheat the oven according to the croissant package instructions. If using fresh croissants, skip this step.

Slice and Toast Croissants (if desired):
- Slice each croissant horizontally without cutting all the way through. Toast the croissants in the oven until they are warm and lightly crispy.

Mix Cream Cheese and Dill:
- In a small bowl, mix the softened cream cheese with chopped fresh dill. This adds a herby flavor to the cream cheese.

Spread Cream Cheese Mixture:
- Spread a generous amount of the cream cheese and dill mixture on the bottom half of each croissant.

Add Smoked Salmon:
- Layer smoked salmon evenly over the cream cheese-covered croissants.

Sprinkle with Toppings:
- Sprinkle chopped red onion and capers over the smoked salmon.

Close the Croissants:
- Close the croissants by placing the top half over the smoked salmon and toppings.

Serve:
- Arrange the smoked salmon and cream cheese croissants on a serving platter.

Garnish and Season (Optional):

- Garnish with additional fresh dill on top. Optionally, add a sprinkle of freshly ground black pepper for extra flavor.

Serve with Lemon Wedges:
- Serve the croissants with lemon wedges on the side. Squeezing a little lemon juice over the smoked salmon adds brightness to the dish.

Enjoy:
- These delightful smoked salmon and cream cheese croissants are ready to be enjoyed. They make for an elegant and delicious brunch or light lunch option.

This recipe combines the rich, smoky flavor of the salmon with the creamy texture of the cheese and the buttery goodness of the croissants for a delightful culinary experience.

Spinach and Mushroom Quiche

Ingredients:

For the Pie Crust:

>1 1/4 cups all-purpose flour
>1/2 cup unsalted butter, chilled and cubed
>1/4 teaspoon salt
>3-4 tablespoons ice water

For the Filling:

5. 1 tablespoon olive oil

>1 small onion, finely chopped
>2 cups fresh spinach, chopped
>1 cup mushrooms, sliced
>3 cloves garlic, minced
>4 large eggs
>1 cup milk
>1 cup shredded Swiss cheese
>Salt and pepper to taste
>1/4 teaspoon nutmeg (optional)

Instructions:

Prepare the Pie Crust:

>Combine Ingredients:
>- In a food processor, combine the flour, chilled butter cubes, and salt. Pulse until the mixture resembles coarse crumbs.
>
>Add Ice Water:
>- With the food processor running, add ice water one tablespoon at a time until the dough comes together. Be careful not to overmix.
>
>Form a Disk:

- Turn the dough out onto a floured surface, gather it into a ball, and flatten into a disk. Wrap in plastic wrap and refrigerate for at least 30 minutes.

Roll Out the Crust:
- Preheat the oven to 375°F (190°C). Roll out the chilled dough on a floured surface and fit it into a 9-inch pie dish. Trim any excess and crimp the edges.

Pre-Bake the Crust:
- Line the pie crust with parchment paper and fill it with pie weights or dried beans. Bake for about 15 minutes. Remove the weights and parchment, then bake for an additional 5 minutes until the crust is lightly golden. Set aside.

Prepare the Filling:

Sauté Vegetables:
- In a skillet, heat olive oil over medium heat. Sauté onions until translucent, then add mushrooms and garlic. Cook until the mushrooms release their moisture and the mixture is slightly dry. Add chopped spinach and cook until wilted. Allow the mixture to cool slightly.

Whisk Eggs and Milk:
- In a bowl, whisk together eggs, milk, salt, pepper, and nutmeg (if using).

Assemble the Quiche:
- Spread the sautéed vegetable mixture evenly over the pre-baked pie crust. Pour the egg and milk mixture over the vegetables. Sprinkle shredded Swiss cheese on top.

Bake:
- Bake in the preheated oven for 35-40 minutes or until the quiche is set and the top is golden brown.

Cool and Serve:
- Allow the quiche to cool for a few minutes before slicing. Serve warm and enjoy a slice of this flavorful spinach and mushroom quiche.

This quiche is a perfect option for brunch or a light dinner, combining the earthy flavors of mushrooms and spinach with the creamy richness of eggs and Swiss cheese.

Cheddar and Chive Biscuits with Sausage Gravy

Ingredients:

For the Biscuits:

    2 cups all-purpose flour
    1 tablespoon baking powder
    1/2 teaspoon baking soda
    1/2 teaspoon salt
    1/2 cup unsalted butter, cold and cubed
    1 cup sharp cheddar cheese, shredded
    1/4 cup fresh chives, chopped
    1 cup buttermilk

For the Sausage Gravy:

9. 1 pound breakfast sausage (pork or turkey)

    1/4 cup all-purpose flour
    3 cups whole milk
    Salt and black pepper to taste
    Pinch of cayenne pepper (optional)

Instructions:

Make the Biscuits:

    Preheat Oven:
- Preheat the oven to 450°F (230°C).

    Combine Dry Ingredients:
- In a large bowl, whisk together the flour, baking powder, baking soda, and salt.

    Cut in Butter:
- Add the cold, cubed butter to the dry ingredients. Use a pastry cutter or your fingers to cut the butter into the flour until the mixture resembles coarse crumbs.

Add Cheese and Chives:
- Stir in the shredded cheddar cheese and chopped chives.

Pour in Buttermilk:
- Make a well in the center of the mixture and pour in the buttermilk. Stir until just combined.

Shape and Cut Biscuits:
- Turn the dough out onto a floured surface. Pat it into a rectangle and fold it over itself a few times. Roll or pat the dough to about 1-inch thickness. Cut out biscuits using a round cutter.

Bake:
- Place the biscuits on a baking sheet lined with parchment paper. Bake for 12-15 minutes or until golden brown.

Prepare the Sausage Gravy:

Cook Sausage:
- In a large skillet over medium heat, cook the breakfast sausage, breaking it into crumbles as it cooks. Once cooked through, remove excess grease, leaving about 2 tablespoons in the pan.

Make Roux:
- Sprinkle flour over the cooked sausage and stir to create a roux. Cook for 1-2 minutes to eliminate the raw flour taste.

Gradually Add Milk:
- Gradually add the milk to the skillet, stirring constantly to avoid lumps. Bring the mixture to a simmer.

Season and Thicken:
- Season with salt, black pepper, and cayenne pepper (if using). Allow the gravy to simmer until it thickens to your desired consistency.

Serve:
- Split the warm cheddar and chive biscuits and spoon the sausage gravy over the top. Serve immediately and enjoy this hearty and comforting dish.

This recipe combines the flaky goodness of cheddar and chive biscuits with the savory richness of sausage gravy for a classic and satisfying breakfast or brunch dish.

Blueberry Almond French Toast Casserole

Ingredients:

For the Casserole:

    1 loaf of French bread, cut into 1-inch cubes
    1 cup fresh or frozen blueberries
    8 large eggs
    2 cups milk
    1/2 cup heavy cream
    1/2 cup granulated sugar
    1 teaspoon vanilla extract
    1/2 teaspoon almond extract
    1/2 teaspoon ground cinnamon
    1/4 teaspoon salt

For the Almond Streusel Topping:

11. 1/2 cup all-purpose flour

    1/4 cup brown sugar, packed
    1/4 cup cold unsalted butter, cubed
    1/2 cup sliced almonds
    Powdered sugar for dusting (optional)

Instructions:

Prepare the Casserole:

    Preheat Oven:
- Preheat the oven to 350°F (175°C). Grease a 9x13-inch baking dish.

    Layer Ingredients:
- Spread half of the cubed French bread in the prepared baking dish. Sprinkle half of the blueberries over the bread. Repeat with the remaining bread and blueberries.

    Whisk Wet Ingredients:
- In a large bowl, whisk together the eggs, milk, heavy cream, granulated sugar, vanilla extract, almond extract, ground cinnamon, and salt.

    Pour Mixture Over Bread:

- Pour the egg mixture evenly over the bread and blueberries in the baking dish, making sure all the bread is coated. Press down gently to help the bread absorb the liquid.

Refrigerate:
- Cover the baking dish with plastic wrap and refrigerate for at least 1 hour, or overnight for best results, to allow the bread to soak up the liquid.

Make the Almond Streusel Topping:

Combine Ingredients:
- In a medium bowl, combine the flour, brown sugar, cold cubed butter, and sliced almonds. Use your fingers to crumble the mixture until it resembles coarse crumbs.

Bake the Casserole:

Sprinkle Streusel Topping:
- Sprinkle the almond streusel topping evenly over the soaked bread mixture.

Bake:
- Bake in the preheated oven for 45-50 minutes or until the top is golden brown and the center is set.

Cool and Serve:
- Allow the casserole to cool for a few minutes before serving. Optionally, dust with powdered sugar before serving.

Serve:
- Serve warm slices of the Blueberry Almond French Toast Casserole with maple syrup if desired.

This delightful casserole combines the sweet burst of blueberries, the nutty flavor of almonds, and the richness of French toast for a delicious and comforting breakfast or brunch dish.

Breakfast Tostadas with Avocado and Fried Eggs

Ingredients:

    4 corn tostadas
    2 ripe avocados, mashed
    4 large eggs
    1 tablespoon olive oil
    Salt and black pepper to taste
    1 cup cherry tomatoes, halved
    1/4 cup red onion, finely chopped
    Fresh cilantro, chopped, for garnish
    Lime wedges for serving

Optional Toppings:

- Salsa
- Shredded cheese
- Hot sauce
- Sour cream

Instructions:

Prepare the Avocado Spread:
- In a bowl, mash the ripe avocados. Season with salt and black pepper to taste. Set aside.

Fry the Eggs:
- In a non-stick skillet, heat olive oil over medium heat. Crack the eggs into the skillet and cook to your liking (fried or sunny-side-up). Season with salt and black pepper.

Assemble the Tostadas:
- Spread a generous amount of mashed avocado onto each tostada.

Add Fried Eggs:
- Place a fried egg on top of the mashed avocado on each tostada.

Top with Fresh Vegetables:
- Sprinkle halved cherry tomatoes and chopped red onion over the fried eggs.

Garnish:

- Garnish the breakfast tostadas with fresh cilantro.

Optional Toppings:
- Add additional toppings like salsa, shredded cheese, hot sauce, or sour cream according to your preference.

Serve with Lime Wedges:
- Serve the breakfast tostadas with lime wedges on the side for squeezing over the top.

Enjoy:
- Serve immediately and enjoy this flavorful and satisfying breakfast dish.

These Breakfast Tostadas with Avocado and Fried Eggs are a delicious and nutritious way to start your day, providing a perfect balance of protein, healthy fats, and fresh vegetables. Customize them with your favorite toppings for added flavor.

Coconut Mango Smoothie Bowl

Ingredients:

For the Smoothie Base:

1 cup frozen mango chunks
1/2 cup frozen pineapple chunks
1 ripe banana, peeled and frozen
1/2 cup coconut milk
1/2 cup Greek yogurt (or dairy-free alternative)
1 tablespoon honey or maple syrup (optional, depending on sweetness preference)

For Toppings:

7. Fresh mango slices

Shredded coconut
Granola
Chia seeds
Sliced banana
Edible flowers (optional)
Nuts or seeds (e.g., sliced almonds, pumpkin seeds)

Instructions:

Prepare Smoothie Base:
- In a blender, combine the frozen mango chunks, frozen pineapple chunks, frozen banana, coconut milk, Greek yogurt, and honey or maple syrup (if using).

Blend Until Smooth:
- Blend the ingredients until smooth and creamy. If needed, add a bit more coconut milk to achieve your desired consistency.

Pour into a Bowl:
- Pour the smoothie into a bowl, ensuring it has a thick consistency suitable for eating with a spoon.

Add Toppings:
- Arrange toppings on the smoothie bowl. Suggestions include fresh mango slices, shredded coconut, granola, chia seeds, sliced banana, nuts or seeds, and edible flowers for a decorative touch.

Serve and Enjoy:
- Serve the Coconut Mango Smoothie Bowl immediately, allowing you to enjoy the vibrant flavors and textures.

Optional Additions:
- Customize your bowl by adding other fruits, such as berries or kiwi, and incorporating additional superfoods like flaxseeds or hemp hearts.

Drizzle with Honey (Optional):
- For an extra touch of sweetness, drizzle a bit of honey over the top of your smoothie bowl.

Enjoy:
- Grab a spoon and enjoy the tropical goodness of this Coconut Mango Smoothie Bowl, perfect for a refreshing breakfast or a healthy snack.

Feel free to experiment with the ingredients and toppings to create your own variations of this delicious and nutritious smoothie bowl.

Ham and Cheese Breakfast Burritos

Ingredients:

4 large flour tortillas
8 large eggs
1/4 cup milk
Salt and black pepper to taste
1 tablespoon butter or oil
1 cup diced cooked ham
1 cup shredded cheddar cheese
1/4 cup diced green onions (optional)
Salsa or hot sauce for serving

Instructions:

Prepare the Eggs:
- In a bowl, whisk together the eggs, milk, salt, and black pepper.

Cook Scrambled Eggs:
- Heat the butter or oil in a large skillet over medium heat. Pour in the egg mixture and scramble the eggs until they are cooked through but still moist. Remove from heat.

Warm the Tortillas:
- Warm the flour tortillas in a dry skillet or microwave them for a few seconds to make them pliable.

Assemble the Burritos:
- Lay out each tortilla and spoon a portion of the scrambled eggs down the center.

Add Ham and Cheese:
- Sprinkle diced ham and shredded cheddar cheese over the eggs.

Optional: Add Green Onions:
- Optionally, add diced green onions for extra flavor.

Fold the Burritos:
- Fold in the sides of the tortilla and then roll it up tightly to create a burrito.

Optional: Heat in Pan (Optional):
- If desired, you can place the assembled burritos in a hot skillet for a minute or two to lightly toast and seal the edges.

Serve with Salsa or Hot Sauce:

- Serve the ham and cheese breakfast burritos with your favorite salsa or hot sauce on the side.

Enjoy:
- Enjoy these delicious and hearty breakfast burritos that are perfect for a quick and satisfying morning meal.

Feel free to customize these breakfast burritos by adding ingredients like sautéed vegetables, avocado slices, or sour cream according to your taste preferences.

Cinnamon Swirl Coffee Cake

Ingredients:

For the Cake:

- 2 cups all-purpose flour
- 1 teaspoon baking powder
- 1/2 teaspoon baking soda
- 1/2 teaspoon salt
- 1/2 cup unsalted butter, softened
- 1 cup granulated sugar
- 2 large eggs
- 1 teaspoon vanilla extract
- 1 cup sour cream

For the Cinnamon Swirl:

10. 1/2 cup brown sugar, packed

- 2 teaspoons ground cinnamon

For the Streusel Topping:

12. 1/2 cup all-purpose flour

- 1/4 cup granulated sugar
- 1/4 cup unsalted butter, cold and cubed

For the Glaze (Optional):

15. 1/2 cup powdered sugar

- 1-2 tablespoons milk
- 1/2 teaspoon vanilla extract

Instructions:

Preheat Oven:

Preheat the oven to 350°F (175°C). Grease and flour a 9x9-inch baking pan.

Make the Cinnamon Swirl:

2. In a small bowl, mix together the brown sugar and ground cinnamon for the swirl. Set aside.

Prepare the Streusel Topping:

3. In another bowl, combine the flour, granulated sugar, and cold cubed butter. Use a fork or your fingers to create a crumbly streusel mixture. Set aside.

Make the Cake Batter:

4. In a medium bowl, whisk together the flour, baking powder, baking soda, and salt.

- In a large bowl or mixer, cream together the softened butter and granulated sugar until light and fluffy.
- Add the eggs one at a time, beating well after each addition. Stir in the vanilla extract.
- Gradually add the dry ingredients to the wet ingredients, alternating with the sour cream. Begin and end with the dry ingredients.

Assemble the Coffee Cake:

8. Spread half of the cake batter into the prepared baking pan.

- Sprinkle half of the cinnamon swirl mixture over the batter.
- Spoon the remaining cake batter over the swirl mixture.
- Swirl the batter gently with a knife or spatula.
- Sprinkle the remaining cinnamon swirl mixture on top.
- Finally, sprinkle the streusel topping evenly over the batter.

Bake:

14. Bake in the preheated oven for 45-50 minutes or until a toothpick inserted into the center comes out clean.

> Allow the coffee cake to cool in the pan for about 15 minutes before transferring it to a wire rack to cool completely.

Optional Glaze:

16. If desired, whisk together the powdered sugar, milk, and vanilla extract to make a glaze. Drizzle it over the cooled coffee cake.

Slice and Serve:

17. Once the glaze is set, slice the cinnamon swirl coffee cake into squares and serve. Enjoy the delightful combination of cinnamon, streusel, and moist cake!

This coffee cake is perfect for brunch, afternoon tea, or whenever you want to treat yourself to a delicious and comforting baked good.

Caprese Breakfast Sandwich

Ingredients:

    2 English muffins, split and toasted
    2 large eggs
    4 slices fresh mozzarella cheese
    2 slices of ripe tomato
    Fresh basil leaves
    Balsamic glaze or balsamic reduction
    Salt and black pepper to taste
    Olive oil for cooking

Instructions:

    Prepare the English Muffins:
- Split the English muffins and toast them until golden brown.

    Cook the Eggs:
- In a non-stick skillet, heat a bit of olive oil over medium heat. Crack the eggs into the skillet and cook to your liking (fried or scrambled). Season with salt and black pepper.

    Assemble the Sandwiches:
- Place a slice of fresh mozzarella on the bottom half of each English muffin.

    Add Tomato and Basil:
- Top the mozzarella with a slice of ripe tomato and fresh basil leaves.

    Layer with Cooked Eggs:
- Place the cooked eggs on top of the basil.

    Drizzle with Balsamic Glaze:
- Drizzle balsamic glaze or balsamic reduction over the eggs and assemble the sandwiches by placing the top half of the English muffin.

    Serve:
- Serve the Caprese Breakfast Sandwiches immediately while warm.

    Optional Variation: Avocado (Optional):
- For an extra layer of creaminess, you can add sliced avocado to the sandwich.

    Enjoy:
- Enjoy this fresh and flavorful Caprese Breakfast Sandwich, perfect for a leisurely breakfast or brunch.

This breakfast sandwich combines the classic Caprese flavors of fresh mozzarella, tomato, and basil with eggs on a toasted English muffin, creating a delicious and satisfying morning meal.

Quinoa and Veggie Breakfast Bowl

Ingredients:

For the Quinoa:

    1 cup quinoa, rinsed and drained
    2 cups water or vegetable broth
    Salt to taste

For the Veggie Saute:

4. 1 tablespoon olive oil

    1 bell pepper, diced
    1 zucchini, diced
    1 cup cherry tomatoes, halved
    2 cups fresh spinach leaves
    2 cloves garlic, minced
    Salt and black pepper to taste
    1 teaspoon dried oregano (optional)

For Assembly:

12. Avocado slices

    Poached or fried eggs
    Feta cheese, crumbled (optional)
    Fresh herbs (such as parsley or cilantro), chopped
    Hot sauce or salsa (optional)

Instructions:

Prepare Quinoa:

    Rinse Quinoa:
        - Rinse quinoa under cold water to remove any bitterness.
    Cook Quinoa:

- In a medium saucepan, combine quinoa, water or vegetable broth, and a pinch of salt. Bring to a boil, then reduce heat to low, cover, and simmer for about 15-20 minutes or until the quinoa is cooked and water is absorbed.

Fluff Quinoa:
- Fluff the cooked quinoa with a fork and set aside.

Prepare Veggie Saute:

Saute Veggies:
- In a large skillet, heat olive oil over medium heat. Add diced bell pepper, zucchini, and cherry tomatoes. Cook for 4-5 minutes until vegetables are slightly tender.

Add Spinach and Garlic:
- Add fresh spinach and minced garlic to the skillet. Cook for an additional 2-3 minutes until the spinach wilts.

Season:
- Season the veggies with salt, black pepper, and dried oregano (if using). Stir to combine.

Assemble the Breakfast Bowl:

Layer Quinoa and Veggies:
- In serving bowls, layer the cooked quinoa and the sautéed veggies.

Top with Avocado:
- Add slices of avocado on top.

Add Poached or Fried Eggs:
- Place a poached or fried egg on each bowl.

Garnish:
- Sprinkle crumbled feta cheese (if using) and fresh herbs over the bowls.

Optional: Add Hot Sauce or Salsa:
- Drizzle with hot sauce or salsa for an extra kick.

Serve:
- Serve the Quinoa and Veggie Breakfast Bowl immediately, and enjoy a nutritious and flavorful breakfast.

This breakfast bowl is not only packed with protein and nutrients but also offers a variety of textures and flavors, making it a delicious and satisfying way to start your day.

Chocolate Hazelnut Stuffed Croissants

Ingredients:

1 package of crescent roll dough (8 pieces)
1/2 cup chocolate hazelnut spread (such as Nutella)
1 tablespoon melted butter (for brushing)
Powdered sugar for dusting (optional)

Instructions:

Preheat Oven:
- Preheat your oven according to the crescent roll package instructions.

Unroll Crescent Dough:
- Lay out the crescent roll dough on a clean surface, separating the triangles.

Spread Chocolate Hazelnut:
- Spread a generous layer of chocolate hazelnut spread onto each crescent triangle, covering the surface.

Roll Up Croissants:
- Starting from the wider end, roll each triangle into a crescent shape. Make sure to seal the edges.

Brush with Melted Butter:
- Place the rolled croissants on a baking sheet lined with parchment paper. Brush the tops with melted butter for a golden finish.

Bake:
- Bake in the preheated oven according to the crescent roll package instructions or until the croissants are golden brown and cooked through.

Cool:
- Allow the chocolate hazelnut stuffed croissants to cool slightly on a wire rack.

Optional Dusting:
- If desired, dust the croissants with powdered sugar for an extra touch of sweetness.

Serve:
- Serve the chocolate hazelnut stuffed croissants warm and enjoy!

These delicious treats are a simple and delightful way to enjoy the classic combination of chocolate and hazelnut in a flaky and buttery croissant. Perfect for breakfast, brunch, or a sweet snack.

Greek Yogurt and Berry Parfait

Ingredients:

1 cup Greek yogurt (unsweetened)
1 cup mixed berries (strawberries, blueberries, raspberries)
2 tablespoons honey or maple syrup
1/2 cup granola
1/4 cup chopped nuts (such as almonds or walnuts)
Fresh mint leaves for garnish (optional)

Instructions:

Prepare the Greek Yogurt:
- In a bowl, mix the Greek yogurt with honey or maple syrup. Adjust the sweetness to your liking.

Layer with Berries:
- In serving glasses or bowls, start by adding a layer of Greek yogurt.

Add Mixed Berries:
- Top the yogurt with a layer of mixed berries. You can use a combination of strawberries, blueberries, and raspberries.

Repeat Layers:
- Repeat the layers by adding another layer of Greek yogurt, followed by mixed berries.

Top with Granola:
- Sprinkle a layer of granola over the top. This adds a crunchy texture to the parfait.

Add Chopped Nuts:
- Sprinkle chopped nuts (such as almonds or walnuts) over the granola.

Garnish with Mint (Optional):
- If desired, garnish the parfait with fresh mint leaves for a burst of freshness.

Serve Immediately:
- Serve the Greek Yogurt and Berry Parfait immediately and enjoy the delightful combination of creamy yogurt, sweet berries, and crunchy granola.

This simple and nutritious parfait is not only visually appealing but also a tasty way to start your day or enjoy a healthy snack. Feel free to customize the parfait with your favorite fruits, nuts, or seeds.

Southwest Frittata with Black Beans and Corn

Ingredients:

    8 large eggs
    1/4 cup milk
    1 cup black beans, cooked and drained
    1 cup corn kernels (fresh, frozen, or canned)
    1 red bell pepper, diced
    1 small red onion, finely chopped
    1 cup cherry tomatoes, halved
    1 cup shredded cheddar or Monterey Jack cheese
    1 teaspoon ground cumin
    1 teaspoon chili powder
    Salt and black pepper to taste
    2 tablespoons olive oil
    Fresh cilantro, chopped, for garnish
    Avocado slices for serving (optional)
    Salsa for serving (optional)

Instructions:

    Preheat Oven:
- Preheat your oven broiler.

    Prepare Vegetables:
- In a large oven-safe skillet, heat olive oil over medium heat. Add diced red bell pepper and chopped red onion. Sauté until softened.

    Add Corn and Black Beans:
- Add corn kernels and cooked black beans to the skillet. Stir to combine.

    Season with Spices:
- Sprinkle ground cumin, chili powder, salt, and black pepper over the vegetables. Stir to evenly distribute the spices.

    Whisk Eggs:
- In a bowl, whisk together eggs and milk until well combined.

    Pour Egg Mixture:
- Pour the whisked egg mixture over the vegetables in the skillet. Allow the eggs to set around the edges.

    Add Cherry Tomatoes and Cheese:

- Sprinkle halved cherry tomatoes over the eggs. Sprinkle shredded cheese evenly across the top.

Broil in Oven:
- Place the skillet under the preheated broiler for 3-5 minutes or until the frittata is set and the top is golden brown.

Garnish and Serve:
- Remove the skillet from the oven, garnish with fresh cilantro, and let it cool slightly.

Slice and Serve:
- Slice the Southwest Frittata into wedges and serve. Optionally, top with avocado slices and salsa for extra flavor.

Enjoy:
- Enjoy this flavorful Southwest Frittata as a satisfying breakfast, brunch, or even a light dinner.

Feel free to customize this frittata by adding other ingredients like diced jalapeños, green onions, or a dollop of sour cream. The versatile nature of frittatas allows you to get creative with your favorite Southwest-inspired ingredients.

Banana Walnut Pancakes

Ingredients:

2 cups all-purpose flour
2 tablespoons sugar
2 teaspoons baking powder
1/2 teaspoon baking soda
1/4 teaspoon salt
2 large ripe bananas, mashed
2 large eggs
1 1/2 cups buttermilk
1 teaspoon vanilla extract
1/2 cup chopped walnuts
Butter or oil for cooking
Maple syrup for serving

Instructions:

Prepare Dry Ingredients:
- In a large mixing bowl, whisk together the flour, sugar, baking powder, baking soda, and salt.

Mix Wet Ingredients:
- In a separate bowl, mash the ripe bananas. Add the eggs, buttermilk, and vanilla extract. Mix until well combined.

Combine Wet and Dry Ingredients:
- Pour the wet ingredients into the dry ingredients. Stir until just combined. Do not overmix; a few lumps are okay.

Add Chopped Walnuts:
- Gently fold in the chopped walnuts into the pancake batter.

Preheat Griddle or Pan:
- Preheat a griddle or non-stick pan over medium heat. Add a small amount of butter or oil to coat the surface.

Spoon Batter onto Griddle:
- Using a 1/4 cup measuring cup, spoon the pancake batter onto the griddle. Spread it slightly with the back of the cup.

Cook Until Bubbles Form:

- Cook until bubbles form on the surface of the pancake and the edges start to look set.

Flip and Cook Other Side:
- Carefully flip the pancake and cook the other side until golden brown.

Repeat:
- Repeat the process with the remaining batter, adding more butter or oil to the griddle as needed.

Keep Warm:
- Keep the cooked pancakes warm in a low oven until ready to serve.

Serve with Maple Syrup:
- Serve the Banana Walnut Pancakes warm with a drizzle of maple syrup.

Enjoy:
- Enjoy these delicious and fluffy pancakes with the delightful combination of bananas and walnuts.

These Banana Walnut Pancakes are a delightful twist on classic pancakes, incorporating the natural sweetness of ripe bananas and the crunch of chopped walnuts. Perfect for a cozy breakfast or brunch treat!

Bacon and Hash Brown Breakfast Skillet

Ingredients:

    6 slices bacon, chopped
    4 cups frozen hash browns, thawed
    1 onion, finely chopped
    1 bell pepper, diced (any color)
    1 cup shredded cheddar cheese
    4 large eggs
    Salt and black pepper to taste
    Chopped fresh parsley or green onions for garnish (optional)

Instructions:

    Cook Bacon:
- In a large skillet over medium heat, cook the chopped bacon until it becomes crispy. Remove bacon from the skillet and set it aside on a paper towel-lined plate.

    Cook Hash Browns:
- In the same skillet with the bacon drippings, add the thawed hash browns. Cook until they become golden brown and crispy on the edges, following the package instructions.

    Add Onion and Bell Pepper:
- Add the finely chopped onion and diced bell pepper to the skillet. Sauté until the vegetables are softened.

    Combine Bacon and Cheese:
- Return the cooked bacon to the skillet. Sprinkle shredded cheddar cheese over the hash browns, bacon, and vegetables. Allow the cheese to melt.

    Make Indentations for Eggs:
- Using a spoon, make indentations in the hash brown mixture for the eggs.

    Crack Eggs into Indentations:
- Crack one egg into each indentation. Season the eggs with salt and black pepper to taste.

    Cover and Cook:
- Cover the skillet and cook until the eggs are cooked to your liking (runny or set). This usually takes about 5-7 minutes.

    Garnish and Serve:

- Garnish the breakfast skillet with chopped fresh parsley or green onions, if desired.

Serve Warm:
- Serve the Bacon and Hash Brown Breakfast Skillet warm directly from the skillet, allowing everyone to dig in and enjoy.

Optional: Bake in Oven (Optional):
- If you prefer, you can transfer the skillet to a preheated oven (375°F or 190°C) and bake until the eggs are cooked to your liking.

Enjoy:
- Enjoy this hearty and flavorful breakfast skillet that combines the goodness of crispy bacon, hash browns, melted cheese, and perfectly cooked eggs.

This Bacon and Hash Brown Breakfast Skillet is a delicious and satisfying breakfast or brunch option that brings together classic breakfast elements in a single, flavorful dish.

Avocado and Tomato Breakfast Tacos

Ingredients:

4 small flour or corn tortillas
2 ripe avocados, sliced
1 cup cherry tomatoes, halved
4 large eggs
1 tablespoon olive oil
Salt and black pepper to taste
1/2 teaspoon cumin powder
1/2 cup crumbled feta or cotija cheese
Fresh cilantro, chopped, for garnish
Lime wedges for serving

Instructions:

Prepare Tortillas:
- Warm the tortillas in a dry skillet or microwave according to the package instructions.

Cook Eggs:
- In a non-stick skillet, heat olive oil over medium heat. Crack the eggs into the skillet and cook to your liking (fried or scrambled). Season with salt, black pepper, and cumin powder.

Assemble Tacos:
- On each tortilla, place slices of ripe avocado.

Add Cooked Eggs:
- Top the avocado with the cooked eggs.

Add Tomatoes:
- Scatter halved cherry tomatoes over the eggs.

Sprinkle with Cheese:
- Sprinkle crumbled feta or cotija cheese over the tacos.

Garnish:
- Garnish with chopped fresh cilantro for a burst of flavor.

Serve with Lime Wedges:
- Serve the Avocado and Tomato Breakfast Tacos with lime wedges on the side for squeezing over the top.

Optional Additions:

- Customize your tacos by adding ingredients like salsa, hot sauce, diced onions, or sour cream according to your preference.

Enjoy:
- Enjoy these delicious and fresh Avocado and Tomato Breakfast Tacos for a wholesome and satisfying morning meal.

These breakfast tacos are a quick and tasty way to enjoy the vibrant flavors of avocado and tomato. Feel free to get creative with additional toppings and make it your own!

Lemon Blueberry Muffins

Ingredients:

For the Muffins:

    2 cups all-purpose flour
    1 cup granulated sugar
    1 tablespoon baking powder
    1/2 teaspoon baking soda
    1/4 teaspoon salt
    1 cup plain Greek yogurt
    2 large eggs
    1/2 cup unsalted butter, melted
    1 teaspoon vanilla extract
    Zest of 1 lemon
    2 tablespoons fresh lemon juice
    1 1/2 cups fresh or frozen blueberries (if using frozen, do not thaw)

For the Lemon Glaze:

13. 1 cup powdered sugar

    2 tablespoons fresh lemon juice
    Zest of 1 lemon

Instructions:

Preheat Oven:

    Preheat your oven to 375°F (190°C). Line a muffin tin with paper liners or grease it well.

Make the Muffin Batter:

    Mix Dry Ingredients:

- In a large bowl, whisk together the flour, sugar, baking powder, baking soda, and salt.

Prepare Wet Ingredients:
- In another bowl, mix together the Greek yogurt, eggs, melted butter, vanilla extract, lemon zest, and lemon juice.

Combine Wet and Dry Ingredients:
- Pour the wet ingredients into the dry ingredients and gently fold them together until just combined. Be careful not to overmix.

Fold in Blueberries:
- Gently fold in the blueberries until evenly distributed throughout the batter.

Fill Muffin Cups:
- Divide the batter evenly among the muffin cups, filling each about 2/3 full.

Bake the Muffins:

Bake:
- Bake in the preheated oven for 18-20 minutes or until a toothpick inserted into the center of a muffin comes out clean or with a few moist crumbs.

Cool:
- Allow the muffins to cool in the tin for 5 minutes, then transfer them to a wire rack to cool completely.

Make the Lemon Glaze:

Prepare Glaze:
- In a small bowl, whisk together the powdered sugar, fresh lemon juice, and lemon zest until smooth.

Glaze the Muffins:
- Once the muffins are completely cooled, drizzle the lemon glaze over the top of each muffin.

Optional: Zest Garnish (Optional):
- Optionally, sprinkle a bit more lemon zest on top of the glaze for an extra burst of citrus flavor.

Allow Glaze to Set:
- Allow the glaze to set before serving.

Enjoy:

13. Serve these delicious Lemon Blueberry Muffins and enjoy the perfect combination of tart lemon and sweet blueberries in every bite.

Breakfast Pizza with Eggs and Bacon

Ingredients:

For the Pizza Dough:

    1 pound pizza dough (store-bought or homemade)
    Cornmeal or flour (for dusting)

For the Toppings:

3. 1 cup shredded mozzarella cheese

    1 cup cooked and crumbled bacon
    4 large eggs
    Salt and black pepper to taste
    1/4 cup grated Parmesan cheese
    Fresh chives or green onions, chopped (for garnish)

For Optional Extras:

9. Sautéed mushrooms

    Sliced cherry tomatoes
    Sliced bell peppers
    Spinach leaves

Instructions:

Preheat Oven:

    Preheat your oven to the temperature recommended on the pizza dough package or according to your homemade dough recipe.

Prepare Pizza Dough:

If using store-bought pizza dough, let it come to room temperature. On a lightly floured surface, roll out the pizza dough to your desired thickness.
Transfer the rolled-out dough to a pizza stone or a baking sheet dusted with cornmeal or flour.

Assemble Pizza:

Spread a thin layer of shredded mozzarella cheese over the pizza dough, leaving a border around the edges for the crust.
Sprinkle the cooked and crumbled bacon evenly over the cheese.
If desired, add optional toppings like sautéed mushrooms, sliced cherry tomatoes, bell peppers, or spinach leaves.
Create small wells in the toppings for the eggs.
Crack one egg into each well, distributing them evenly across the pizza.
Season the eggs with salt and black pepper to taste.

Bake the Pizza:

Transfer the pizza to the preheated oven and bake according to the pizza dough instructions or until the crust is golden brown, and the eggs are cooked to your liking.
Sprinkle grated Parmesan cheese over the pizza during the last few minutes of baking.

Garnish and Serve:

Once out of the oven, garnish the breakfast pizza with fresh chives or chopped green onions.
Allow the pizza to cool slightly before slicing.

Enjoy:

Serve slices of the Breakfast Pizza with Eggs and Bacon, and enjoy a delicious and hearty breakfast.

Feel free to customize the toppings based on your preferences, and get creative with additional ingredients like avocado slices or a drizzle of hot sauce for an extra kick.

Green Shakshuka with Spinach and Feta

Ingredients:

2 tablespoons olive oil
1 large onion, finely chopped
2 cloves garlic, minced
1 jalapeño or serrano pepper, seeded and finely chopped (optional for heat)
1 teaspoon ground cumin
1 teaspoon ground coriander
1 teaspoon paprika
5 cups fresh spinach leaves, chopped
1 cup fresh cilantro, chopped
1 cup fresh parsley, chopped
1 cup crumbled feta cheese
4-6 large eggs
Salt and black pepper to taste
1 tablespoon lemon juice (optional, for extra brightness)
Warm crusty bread for serving

Instructions:

Sauté Aromatics:
- In a large skillet, heat olive oil over medium heat. Add finely chopped onion and sauté until softened.

Add Garlic and Spices:
- Add minced garlic and chopped jalapeño (if using) to the skillet. Sauté for an additional minute until fragrant. Add ground cumin, ground coriander, and paprika. Stir well to combine.

Add Spinach and Herbs:
- Add chopped fresh spinach, cilantro, and parsley to the skillet. Cook until the spinach wilts and the herbs are softened.

Create Wells and Crack Eggs:
- Make wells in the spinach mixture and crack the eggs into the wells.

Sprinkle with Feta:
- Sprinkle crumbled feta cheese over the entire skillet.

Season and Cover:

- Season the eggs with salt and black pepper. Cover the skillet and cook until the eggs are cooked to your liking (runny or set).

Optional: Drizzle with Lemon Juice:
- If desired, drizzle lemon juice over the shakshuka for an extra burst of brightness.

Serve Warm:
- Serve the Green Shakshuka with warm crusty bread for dipping.

Enjoy:
- Enjoy this flavorful and nutritious Green Shakshuka with Spinach and Feta for a delightful breakfast or brunch.

Feel free to customize this recipe by adding other green vegetables like kale or Swiss chard. The combination of vibrant greens, herbs, and creamy feta makes this shakshuka a delicious and satisfying dish.

Raspberry Cheesecake Stuffed French Toast

Ingredients:

For the Raspberry Cheesecake Filling:

8 ounces cream cheese, softened
1/4 cup powdered sugar
1 teaspoon vanilla extract
1/2 cup fresh raspberries

For the French Toast:

5. 8 slices of thick-cut bread (such as brioche or challah)

4 large eggs
1 cup milk
1 teaspoon vanilla extract
1/2 teaspoon ground cinnamon
Pinch of salt
Butter for cooking

For Topping:

12. Fresh raspberries

Maple syrup
Powdered sugar for dusting

Instructions:

Prepare the Raspberry Cheesecake Filling:

In a bowl, combine softened cream cheese, powdered sugar, and vanilla extract. Mix until smooth.
Gently fold in fresh raspberries. Set aside.

Prepare the French Toast:

> Make a slit in each slice of bread to create a pocket for the filling. Be careful not to cut through the bread completely.
> Spoon the raspberry cheesecake filling into the pockets, distributing it evenly among the slices.
> In a shallow dish, whisk together eggs, milk, vanilla extract, ground cinnamon, and a pinch of salt.
> Dip each stuffed slice of bread into the egg mixture, ensuring it is coated on both sides.
> In a large skillet or griddle, melt butter over medium heat.
> Cook the stuffed French toast until golden brown on both sides, ensuring the filling is heated through and slightly melted.

Serve:

> Transfer the stuffed French toast to serving plates.
> Top with fresh raspberries, a drizzle of maple syrup, and a dusting of powdered sugar.
> Serve warm and enjoy this indulgent Raspberry Cheesecake Stuffed French Toast!

This delightful breakfast treat combines the creaminess of cheesecake with the sweetness of fresh raspberries, all tucked inside golden brown French toast. Perfect for a special brunch or whenever you're in the mood for a decadent morning meal.

Veggie and Goat Cheese Omelette

Ingredients:

- 3 large eggs
- 2 tablespoons milk or water
- Salt and black pepper to taste
- 1 tablespoon olive oil or butter
- 1/4 cup red bell pepper, diced
- 1/4 cup green bell pepper, diced
- 1/4 cup red onion, finely chopped
- 1/4 cup cherry tomatoes, halved
- 2 ounces goat cheese, crumbled
- Fresh herbs (such as chives or parsley), chopped, for garnish

Instructions:

Prep the Vegetables:
- Dice the red and green bell peppers, finely chop the red onion, and halve the cherry tomatoes.

Whisk the Eggs:
- In a bowl, whisk together the eggs, milk or water, salt, and black pepper until well combined.

Sauté Vegetables:
- Heat olive oil or butter in a non-stick skillet over medium heat. Add the diced red and green bell peppers and chopped red onion. Sauté until the vegetables are softened.

Add Cherry Tomatoes:
- Add the halved cherry tomatoes to the skillet and cook for an additional 1-2 minutes.

Pour in the Egg Mixture:
- Pour the whisked egg mixture over the sautéed vegetables, ensuring an even distribution.

Swirl and Cook:
- Swirl the pan to spread the eggs evenly. Allow the eggs to cook undisturbed for a moment, then gently lift the edges with a spatula to let the uncooked eggs flow underneath.

Add Goat Cheese:

- Once the omelette is mostly set but still slightly runny on top, crumble the goat cheese evenly over one-half of the omelette.

Fold and Serve:
- Carefully fold the omelette in half, covering the goat cheese filling. Cook for an additional minute or until the eggs are fully set.

Garnish and Serve:
- Slide the omelette onto a plate, garnish with fresh herbs, and serve immediately.

Enjoy:
- Enjoy this delicious Veggie and Goat Cheese Omelette as a wholesome and satisfying breakfast or brunch option.

Feel free to customize the omelette with your favorite vegetables or herbs. The creamy goat cheese adds a tangy flavor that complements the veggies perfectly.

Apple Cider Donuts

Ingredients:

For the Donuts:

- 2 cups apple cider
- 2 cups all-purpose flour
- 1 1/2 teaspoons baking powder
- 1/2 teaspoon baking soda
- 1/2 teaspoon salt
- 1 teaspoon ground cinnamon
- 1/4 teaspoon ground nutmeg
- 1/4 cup unsalted butter, softened
- 1/2 cup granulated sugar
- 1/2 cup brown sugar, packed
- 2 large eggs
- 1 teaspoon vanilla extract

For the Cinnamon Sugar Coating:

- 1/2 cup granulated sugar
- 1 teaspoon ground cinnamon
- 1/4 cup unsalted butter, melted

Instructions:

Prepare Apple Cider Reduction:

In a small saucepan, heat apple cider over medium heat until it reduces to 1/2 cup. Allow it to cool.

Make the Donuts:

Preheat the oven to 350°F (175°C). Grease a donut pan with butter or cooking spray.

In a medium bowl, whisk together flour, baking powder, baking soda, salt, cinnamon, and nutmeg.

In a large bowl, cream together the softened butter, granulated sugar, and brown sugar until light and fluffy.

Add the eggs one at a time, beating well after each addition. Stir in the vanilla extract.

Gradually add the dry ingredients to the wet ingredients, alternating with the reduced apple cider. Begin and end with the dry ingredients, mixing just until combined.

Spoon the batter into the prepared donut pan, filling each cavity about 2/3 full.

Bake in the preheated oven for 12-15 minutes or until a toothpick inserted into the center comes out clean.

Allow the donuts to cool in the pan for a few minutes before transferring them to a wire rack to cool completely.

Coat with Cinnamon Sugar:

In a small bowl, mix together granulated sugar and ground cinnamon for the coating.

Brush each donut with melted butter, then dip into the cinnamon sugar mixture to coat evenly.

Serve and Enjoy:

Serve the Apple Cider Donuts and savor the delightful combination of apple flavor and warm spices.

These homemade Apple Cider Donuts are a perfect fall treat, capturing the essence of apple orchards and autumn flavors. Enjoy them with a cup of coffee or hot apple cider for a cozy and delicious experience.

Chia Seed Pudding Parfait with Kiwi

Ingredients:

For the Chia Seed Pudding:

    1/4 cup chia seeds
    1 cup almond milk (or any milk of your choice)
    1 tablespoon maple syrup or honey
    1/2 teaspoon vanilla extract

For the Parfait:

    2 kiwis, peeled and sliced
    1/2 cup granola
    1/2 cup Greek yogurt (or plant-based yogurt)

Instructions:

Prepare Chia Seed Pudding:

    In a bowl, mix chia seeds, almond milk, maple syrup or honey, and vanilla extract. Stir well to combine.
    Cover the bowl and refrigerate for at least 2-3 hours or overnight, allowing the chia seeds to absorb the liquid and form a pudding-like consistency.

Assemble the Parfait:

    Once the chia seed pudding is set, it's time to assemble the parfait.
    In serving glasses or bowls, layer the chia seed pudding with slices of kiwi.
    Add a layer of Greek yogurt on top of the chia seed pudding and kiwi slices.
    Sprinkle granola over the yogurt layer.
    Repeat the layers until the glass is filled, finishing with a topping of granola and a few slices of kiwi.
    Optionally, drizzle a bit of maple syrup or honey on top for extra sweetness.

Serve and Enjoy:

Serve the Chia Seed Pudding Parfait with Kiwi immediately and enjoy this delicious and nutritious treat.

This parfait offers a delightful combination of creamy chia seed pudding, tangy kiwi, crunchy granola, and smooth Greek yogurt. It's not only a visually appealing breakfast or snack but also a powerhouse of nutrients. Feel free to customize the parfait with your favorite fruits, nuts, or seeds.

Sausage and Pepper Breakfast Burrito

Ingredients:

    4 large flour tortillas
    8 large eggs, scrambled
    1/2 pound breakfast sausage, cooked and crumbled
    1 bell pepper, thinly sliced (any color)
    1 onion, thinly sliced
    1 cup shredded cheddar cheese
    Salt and black pepper to taste
    2 tablespoons olive oil
    Salsa, for serving (optional)
    Fresh cilantro, chopped, for garnish (optional)
    Avocado slices, for serving (optional)

Instructions:

Prepare Sausage and Peppers:

    In a large skillet, heat olive oil over medium heat.
    Add thinly sliced bell pepper and onion to the skillet. Sauté until the vegetables are softened and slightly caramelized.
    Add cooked and crumbled breakfast sausage to the skillet. Stir to combine with the peppers and onions. Cook for an additional 2-3 minutes.
    Season the mixture with salt and black pepper to taste. Remove from heat and set aside.

Scramble Eggs:

    In a separate pan, scramble the eggs over medium-low heat until they are just set.
    Once the eggs are cooked, combine them with the sausage and pepper mixture. Mix well to ensure an even distribution of ingredients.

Assemble Breakfast Burritos:

    Warm the flour tortillas in a dry skillet or microwave.
    Lay out each tortilla and spoon a portion of the sausage, pepper, and egg mixture onto the center.

Sprinkle shredded cheddar cheese on top of the mixture.
Optional: Add salsa, chopped cilantro, and avocado slices for extra flavor.
Fold the sides of the tortilla inwards and then roll it up from the bottom to create a burrito.

Serve:

Place the breakfast burritos seam-side down on a serving plate.
Optionally, garnish with additional salsa, chopped cilantro, or serve with avocado slices on the side.
Serve the Sausage and Pepper Breakfast Burritos warm and enjoy a delicious and satisfying breakfast.

These breakfast burritos are a perfect combination of savory sausage, flavorful peppers, cheesy eggs, and all the goodness wrapped in a tortilla. Customize them with your favorite toppings and enjoy a hearty start to your day!

Peanut Butter Banana Pancakes

Ingredients:

    1 cup all-purpose flour
    1 tablespoon sugar
    1 teaspoon baking powder
    1/2 teaspoon baking soda
    1/4 teaspoon salt
    1 ripe banana, mashed
    1/2 cup creamy peanut butter
    1 cup buttermilk
    1 large egg
    2 tablespoons unsalted butter, melted
    1 teaspoon vanilla extract
    Cooking spray or additional butter for greasing the pan
    Sliced bananas, chopped peanuts, and maple syrup for serving (optional)

Instructions:

    Preheat Griddle or Pan:
- Preheat a griddle or non-stick pan over medium heat. If using a griddle, aim for 350°F (175°C).

    Whisk Dry Ingredients:
- In a large bowl, whisk together the flour, sugar, baking powder, baking soda, and salt.

    Prepare Wet Ingredients:
- In another bowl, mash the ripe banana and mix it with peanut butter, buttermilk, egg, melted butter, and vanilla extract.

    Combine Wet and Dry Ingredients:
- Pour the wet ingredients into the dry ingredients. Stir until just combined. It's okay if the batter has some lumps.

    Cook Pancakes:
- Lightly grease the griddle or pan with cooking spray or butter. Pour 1/4 cup of batter onto the griddle for each pancake.

    Cook Until Bubbles Form:
- Cook until bubbles form on the surface of the pancake and the edges start to look set.

Flip and Cook Other Side:
- Carefully flip the pancake and cook the other side until golden brown.

Repeat:
- Repeat the process with the remaining batter, adding more cooking spray or butter to the griddle as needed.

Keep Warm:
- Keep the cooked pancakes warm in a low oven until ready to serve.

Serve:
- Serve the Peanut Butter Banana Pancakes with sliced bananas, chopped peanuts, and maple syrup if desired.

Enjoy:
- Enjoy these delicious and fluffy pancakes that combine the classic flavors of peanut butter and banana.

These pancakes offer a delightful twist on the traditional stack, incorporating the rich taste of peanut butter and the natural sweetness of ripe bananas. Perfect for a satisfying and indulgent breakfast!

Tomato Basil Bruschetta with Poached Eggs

Ingredients:

For the Bruschetta:

    4-6 slices of rustic bread (baguette or ciabatta)
    2 cups ripe tomatoes, diced
    1/4 cup fresh basil, chopped
    2 cloves garlic, minced
    2 tablespoons extra-virgin olive oil
    Salt and black pepper to taste
    Balsamic glaze for drizzling (optional)

For the Poached Eggs:

    4 large eggs
    1 tablespoon white vinegar (for poaching water)
    Salt and black pepper to taste

Optional Garnish:

    Grated Parmesan cheese
    Fresh basil leaves

Instructions:

Prepare the Bruschetta:

    In a bowl, combine diced tomatoes, chopped fresh basil, minced garlic, and extra-virgin olive oil. Mix well.
    Season the bruschetta mixture with salt and black pepper to taste. Set aside to let the flavors meld.

Toast the Bread:

Toast the slices of rustic bread until golden brown. You can use a toaster, oven, or grill.
Once toasted, rub each slice of bread with a garlic clove for added flavor.

Poach the Eggs:

Fill a large, shallow pan with water. Add white vinegar and bring the water to a gentle simmer.
Crack each egg into a small bowl.
Create a gentle whirlpool in the simmering water and carefully slide each egg into the center. Poach the eggs for about 3-4 minutes for a runny yolk or longer if you prefer a firmer yolk.
Use a slotted spoon to remove the poached eggs from the water and place them on a plate lined with paper towels to absorb excess water.

Assemble the Dish:

Arrange the toasted bread on serving plates.
Spoon generous amounts of the tomato basil bruschetta over each slice.
Carefully place a poached egg on top of the bruschetta on each slice of bread.
Drizzle with balsamic glaze if desired.

Garnish and Serve:

Garnish with grated Parmesan cheese and fresh basil leaves.
Season with additional salt and black pepper if needed.
Serve the Tomato Basil Bruschetta with Poached Eggs immediately for a delightful and flavorful breakfast or brunch.

This dish combines the freshness of tomato basil bruschetta with the richness of perfectly poached eggs, creating a delicious and satisfying meal. Enjoy the contrast of textures and flavors with each bite!

Strawberry Shortcake Waffles

Ingredients:

For the Waffles:

    2 cups all-purpose flour
    1/4 cup granulated sugar
    1 tablespoon baking powder
    1/2 teaspoon salt
    2 large eggs
    1 3/4 cups milk
    1/3 cup vegetable oil
    1 teaspoon vanilla extract

For the Strawberry Topping:

    2 cups fresh strawberries, hulled and sliced
    2 tablespoons granulated sugar
    Whipped cream for serving
    Mint leaves for garnish (optional)

Instructions:

Prepare the Strawberry Topping:

    In a bowl, combine the sliced strawberries and granulated sugar. Toss gently to coat the strawberries in sugar.
    Allow the strawberries to macerate for at least 15-20 minutes, letting them release their juices and create a sweet syrup.

Make the Waffle Batter:

    Preheat your waffle iron according to the manufacturer's instructions.
    In a large bowl, whisk together the flour, sugar, baking powder, and salt.
    In a separate bowl, whisk together the eggs, milk, vegetable oil, and vanilla extract.
    Pour the wet ingredients into the dry ingredients and stir until just combined. Be careful not to overmix; a few lumps are okay.

Cook the Waffles:

- Lightly grease the waffle iron with cooking spray or a small amount of oil.
- Pour the waffle batter onto the preheated iron, spreading it evenly.
- Close the waffle iron and cook according to the manufacturer's instructions until the waffles are golden brown and crisp.
- Repeat until all the batter is used.

Assemble the Strawberry Shortcake Waffles:

- Place a waffle on a serving plate.
- Spoon the macerated strawberries over the waffle.
- Top with a generous dollop of whipped cream.
- Optionally, garnish with mint leaves for a fresh touch.
- Repeat with the remaining waffles.

Serve and Enjoy:

- Serve the Strawberry Shortcake Waffles immediately, allowing everyone to enjoy this delightful and decadent breakfast treat.

These Strawberry Shortcake Waffles are a perfect combination of fluffy waffles, sweet macerated strawberries, and airy whipped cream. They make for a delightful breakfast or brunch that captures the essence of a classic strawberry shortcake.

Mediterranean Quinoa Salad with Poached Eggs

Ingredients:

For the Quinoa Salad:

    1 cup quinoa, rinsed and cooked according to package instructions
    1 cup cherry tomatoes, halved
    1 cucumber, diced
    1/2 cup Kalamata olives, pitted and sliced
    1/2 cup red onion, finely chopped
    1/2 cup feta cheese, crumbled
    1/4 cup fresh parsley, chopped
    1/4 cup fresh mint, chopped
    2 tablespoons extra-virgin olive oil
    1 tablespoon red wine vinegar
    Salt and black pepper to taste
    Lemon wedges for serving (optional)

For the Poached Eggs:

    4 large eggs
    1 tablespoon white vinegar (for poaching water)
    Salt and black pepper to taste

Instructions:

Prepare the Quinoa Salad:

    In a large bowl, combine cooked quinoa, cherry tomatoes, cucumber, Kalamata olives, red onion, feta cheese, parsley, and mint.
    In a small bowl, whisk together extra-virgin olive oil, red wine vinegar, salt, and black pepper.
    Drizzle the dressing over the quinoa salad and toss gently to combine. Ensure that the ingredients are well coated.
    Taste and adjust the seasoning if necessary.

Poach the Eggs:

Fill a large, shallow pan with water. Add white vinegar and bring the water to a gentle simmer.
Crack each egg into a small bowl.
Create a gentle whirlpool in the simmering water and carefully slide each egg into the center. Poach the eggs for about 3-4 minutes for a runny yolk or longer if you prefer a firmer yolk.
Use a slotted spoon to remove the poached eggs from the water and place them on a plate lined with paper towels to absorb excess water.

Assemble the Dish:

Divide the Mediterranean Quinoa Salad among serving plates.
Carefully place a poached egg on top of each portion.
Optionally, garnish with additional fresh herbs, a drizzle of olive oil, and lemon wedges for a burst of citrus flavor.

Serve and Enjoy:

Serve the Mediterranean Quinoa Salad with Poached Eggs immediately and enjoy a healthy, flavorful, and protein-packed meal.

This dish combines the vibrant flavors of the Mediterranean with the protein goodness of poached eggs over a bed of quinoa. It's a nutritious and satisfying meal that works well for breakfast, brunch, or a light lunch.

Breakfast BLT Wrap

Ingredients:

4 large whole wheat or spinach tortillas
8 slices bacon, cooked until crispy
4 large eggs, scrambled
1 cup cherry tomatoes, halved
1 cup baby spinach leaves
1 avocado, sliced
1/4 cup mayonnaise
1 tablespoon Dijon mustard
Salt and black pepper to taste

Instructions:

Prepare the Ingredients:
- Cook the bacon until crispy, scramble the eggs, halve the cherry tomatoes, and slice the avocado.

Make the Sauce:
- In a small bowl, mix mayonnaise and Dijon mustard. Season with salt and black pepper to taste. Set aside.

Warm the Tortillas:
- Warm the tortillas in a dry skillet or microwave according to package instructions.

Assemble the Breakfast BLT Wraps:
- Lay out each tortilla on a flat surface.

Spread Sauce:
- Spread a thin layer of the mayo-Dijon sauce over each tortilla.

Add Spinach:
- Place a handful of baby spinach leaves in the center of each tortilla.

Layer Bacon, Eggs, and Veggies:
- Add 2 slices of crispy bacon, a portion of scrambled eggs, halved cherry tomatoes, and slices of avocado on top of the spinach.

Fold and Roll:
- Carefully fold in the sides of the tortilla and then roll it up tightly from the bottom, creating a wrap.

Serve or Cut in Half:

- Optionally, secure the wraps with toothpicks and cut them in half diagonally for easier handling.

Enjoy:
- Serve the Breakfast BLT Wraps immediately, and enjoy a delicious and satisfying breakfast or brunch.

This Breakfast BLT Wrap combines the classic flavors of a BLT sandwich with the addition of scrambled eggs and avocado, making it a hearty and flavorful morning meal. Feel free to customize the ingredients based on your preferences.

Pumpkin Spice Muffins

Ingredients:

Dry Ingredients:

    2 cups all-purpose flour
    1 teaspoon baking powder
    1/2 teaspoon baking soda
    1/2 teaspoon salt
    2 teaspoons ground cinnamon
    1/2 teaspoon ground nutmeg
    1/2 teaspoon ground ginger
    1/4 teaspoon ground cloves

Wet Ingredients:

    1 cup canned pumpkin puree
    1 cup granulated sugar
    1/2 cup brown sugar, packed
    1/2 cup vegetable oil or melted butter
    2 large eggs
    1 teaspoon vanilla extract

Optional Add-ins:

    1/2 cup chopped nuts (such as pecans or walnuts)
    1/2 cup raisins or chocolate chips

Instructions:

Preheat the Oven:
- Preheat your oven to 350°F (175°C). Line a muffin tin with paper liners or grease the cups.

Mix Dry Ingredients:
- In a large bowl, whisk together the flour, baking powder, baking soda, salt, cinnamon, nutmeg, ginger, and cloves. Set aside.

Combine Wet Ingredients:
- In another bowl, whisk together the pumpkin puree, granulated sugar, brown sugar, vegetable oil or melted butter, eggs, and vanilla extract until well combined.

Combine Wet and Dry Mixtures:
- Pour the wet ingredients into the bowl with the dry ingredients. Gently fold the mixture together until just combined. Be careful not to overmix.

Add Optional Add-ins:
- If using, fold in the chopped nuts, raisins, or chocolate chips.

Fill Muffin Cups:
- Spoon the batter into the prepared muffin cups, filling each about 2/3 full.

Bake:
- Bake in the preheated oven for 18-20 minutes or until a toothpick inserted into the center of a muffin comes out clean.

Cool:
- Allow the muffins to cool in the tin for a few minutes, then transfer them to a wire rack to cool completely.

Serve and Enjoy:
- Once cooled, serve the Pumpkin Spice Muffins and enjoy the warm, spiced flavors of fall.

These moist and flavorful Pumpkin Spice Muffins are perfect for breakfast, brunch, or a delightful snack. The combination of aromatic spices and pumpkin creates a cozy and comforting treat, especially during the autumn season.

Bacon and Egg Breakfast Quesadilla

Ingredients:

2 large flour tortillas
4 large eggs, scrambled
8 slices bacon, cooked until crispy
1 cup shredded cheddar cheese
1/2 cup diced tomatoes
1/4 cup diced red onion
Fresh cilantro, chopped, for garnish (optional)
Salt and black pepper to taste
Cooking spray or butter for cooking

Instructions:

Cook Bacon:
- Cook the bacon until crispy, then drain on paper towels and crumble into pieces.

Scramble Eggs:
- In a bowl, scramble the eggs and season with salt and black pepper to taste.

Prepare Quesadilla:
- Lay out one flour tortilla on a flat surface.

Layer Ingredients:
- On half of the tortilla, evenly distribute half of the shredded cheddar cheese, scrambled eggs, crumbled bacon, diced tomatoes, and red onion.

Fold and Press:
- Fold the other half of the tortilla over the ingredients, creating a half-moon shape. Press down gently.

Cook Quesadilla:
- Heat a skillet or griddle over medium heat and lightly coat with cooking spray or butter.
- Place the quesadilla on the skillet and cook for 2-3 minutes on each side or until the tortilla is golden brown and the cheese is melted.

Repeat:
- Repeat the process for the second quesadilla.

Slice and Garnish:

- Once cooked, transfer the quesadillas to a cutting board and let them rest for a moment before slicing into wedges.

Garnish and Serve:
- Garnish with chopped cilantro if desired.

Serve Warm:
- Serve the Bacon and Egg Breakfast Quesadilla warm and enjoy a delicious and savory breakfast.

This breakfast quesadilla combines the classic flavors of bacon and eggs with the goodness of melted cheese, tomatoes, and red onions. It's a satisfying and easy-to-make morning meal that's perfect for breakfast or brunch.

Berry Protein Smoothie Bowl

Ingredients:

For the Smoothie Bowl:

    1 cup mixed berries (strawberries, blueberries, raspberries)
    1 ripe banana, frozen
    1/2 cup Greek yogurt
    1/2 cup almond milk (or any milk of your choice)
    1 scoop vanilla protein powder
    1 tablespoon chia seeds (optional, for added texture)
    Ice cubes (optional)

For Toppings:

    Granola
    Sliced strawberries
    Blueberries
    Shredded coconut
    Chopped nuts (such as almonds or walnuts)
    Honey or maple syrup for drizzling

Instructions:

Prepare the Smoothie Base:
- In a blender, combine the mixed berries, frozen banana, Greek yogurt, almond milk, protein powder, and chia seeds (if using).

Blend Until Smooth:
- Blend the ingredients until smooth and creamy. If the mixture is too thick, you can add more almond milk to achieve the desired consistency.

Adjust Sweetness:
- Taste the smoothie and adjust sweetness if needed. You can add a bit of honey or maple syrup if desired.

Assemble the Smoothie Bowl:
- Pour the smoothie into a bowl.

Add Toppings:

- Arrange the granola, sliced strawberries, blueberries, shredded coconut, and chopped nuts on top of the smoothie.

Drizzle with Honey or Maple Syrup:
- Drizzle a bit of honey or maple syrup over the toppings for extra sweetness.

Serve Immediately:
- Serve the Berry Protein Smoothie Bowl immediately and enjoy a delicious and nutritious breakfast or snack.

This smoothie bowl is not only packed with the goodness of mixed berries and protein but also offers a delightful combination of textures with the crunchy granola and nuts.

It's a refreshing and energizing way to start your day!

Asparagus and Swiss Cheese Strata

Ingredients:

1 pound asparagus, tough ends trimmed, and cut into 1-inch pieces
8 slices day-old bread, cubed (about 4 cups)
1 1/2 cups shredded Swiss cheese
1/2 cup grated Parmesan cheese
8 large eggs
2 1/2 cups milk
1 tablespoon Dijon mustard
1 teaspoon salt
1/2 teaspoon black pepper
1/4 teaspoon nutmeg (optional)
2 tablespoons unsalted butter, melted
Fresh chives, chopped, for garnish (optional)

Instructions:

Preheat the Oven:
- Preheat your oven to 350°F (175°C). Grease a 9x13-inch baking dish.

Blanch Asparagus:
- Bring a pot of salted water to a boil. Add the asparagus pieces and blanch for 2-3 minutes until just tender. Drain and rinse with cold water to stop the cooking process.

Assemble the Strata:
- In the prepared baking dish, layer the cubed bread, blanched asparagus, shredded Swiss cheese, and grated Parmesan cheese.

Whisk the Egg Mixture:
- In a large bowl, whisk together the eggs, milk, Dijon mustard, salt, black pepper, and nutmeg (if using) until well combined.

Pour Egg Mixture Over Layers:
- Pour the egg mixture evenly over the layers in the baking dish. Press down gently with a spatula to ensure the bread absorbs the liquid.

Let it Sit:
- Allow the strata to sit for about 15-20 minutes to let the bread soak up the egg mixture.

Drizzle with Melted Butter:

- Drizzle the melted butter over the top of the strata.

Bake:
- Bake in the preheated oven for 45-50 minutes or until the top is golden brown and the center is set.

Rest Before Serving:
- Let the strata rest for 5-10 minutes before serving. This allows it to set and makes it easier to cut into portions.

Garnish and Serve:
- Garnish with chopped fresh chives if desired. Serve the Asparagus and Swiss Cheese Strata warm, and enjoy a delicious brunch or breakfast casserole.

This Asparagus and Swiss Cheese Strata is a delightful combination of savory flavors, making it a perfect dish for a weekend brunch or special occasion breakfast. The layers of bread, asparagus, and cheese baked in an egg mixture create a comforting and satisfying meal.

Cranberry Orange Scones

Ingredients:

For the Scones:

    2 cups all-purpose flour
    1/3 cup granulated sugar
    1 tablespoon baking powder
    1/2 teaspoon salt
    1/2 cup unsalted butter, cold and cubed
    1/2 cup dried cranberries
    Zest of one orange
    3/4 cup buttermilk
    1 teaspoon vanilla extract

For the Glaze:

    1 cup powdered sugar
    2 tablespoons fresh orange juice
    Zest of one orange (optional)

Instructions:

Prepare the Scones:

    Preheat your oven to 400°F (200°C) and line a baking sheet with parchment paper.
    In a large bowl, whisk together the flour, sugar, baking powder, and salt.
    Add the cold, cubed butter to the dry ingredients. Use a pastry cutter or your fingers to cut the butter into the flour until the mixture resembles coarse crumbs.
    Stir in the dried cranberries and orange zest.
    In a separate bowl, combine the buttermilk and vanilla extract.
    Make a well in the center of the dry ingredients and pour in the buttermilk mixture. Gently stir until just combined. Do not overmix.
    Turn the dough out onto a floured surface and knead it a few times to bring it together. Pat the dough into a circle about 1 inch thick.

Use a sharp knife to cut the circle into 8 wedges.
Place the scones on the prepared baking sheet, leaving some space between each.
Bake for 15-18 minutes or until the scones are golden brown.

Prepare the Glaze:

While the scones are baking, prepare the glaze. In a bowl, whisk together the powdered sugar and fresh orange juice until smooth.
Once the scones are done baking, allow them to cool for a few minutes on the baking sheet.
Drizzle the glaze over the warm scones.
Optionally, sprinkle additional orange zest on top of the glaze for extra flavor.

Serve and Enjoy:

Allow the glaze to set for a few minutes, then serve the Cranberry Orange Scones and enjoy this delightful treat with a cup of tea or coffee.

These scones are perfect for breakfast, brunch, or a sweet afternoon snack. The combination of tart cranberries and citrusy orange in a tender, flaky scone is sure to brighten your day.

Banana Chocolate Chip Waffles

Ingredients:

    2 cups all-purpose flour
    2 tablespoons granulated sugar
    1 tablespoon baking powder
    1/2 teaspoon salt
    2 ripe bananas, mashed
    1 3/4 cups milk
    1/3 cup vegetable oil
    2 large eggs
    1 teaspoon vanilla extract
    1/2 cup chocolate chips
    Cooking spray for greasing the waffle iron

Instructions:

    Preheat Waffle Iron:
- Preheat your waffle iron according to the manufacturer's instructions.

    Mix Dry Ingredients:
- In a large bowl, whisk together the flour, sugar, baking powder, and salt.

    Combine Wet Ingredients:
- In another bowl, mash the ripe bananas and mix them with milk, vegetable oil, eggs, and vanilla extract.

    Create Batter:
- Pour the wet ingredients into the bowl with the dry ingredients. Stir until just combined. Don't overmix; it's okay if there are a few lumps.

    Add Chocolate Chips:
- Gently fold in the chocolate chips into the batter.

    Grease Waffle Iron:
- Lightly coat the waffle iron with cooking spray.

    Cook Waffles:
- Pour the batter onto the preheated waffle iron according to the manufacturer's instructions.

    Cook Until Golden Brown:
- Cook until the waffles are golden brown and crisp.

    Repeat:

- Repeat with the remaining batter.

Serve Warm:
- Serve the Banana Chocolate Chip Waffles warm, either plain or with toppings like sliced bananas, whipped cream, or maple syrup.

Enjoy:
- Enjoy these delicious and flavorful waffles for breakfast or brunch.

These Banana Chocolate Chip Waffles are a delightful twist on traditional waffles, offering a sweet and fruity flavor with the added richness of chocolate. They make for a perfect breakfast or weekend brunch treat.

Bagel with Lox and Cream Cheese

Ingredients:

    1 everything bagel (or your favorite type of bagel)
    4 ounces smoked salmon (lox)
    4 tablespoons cream cheese, softened
    1 tablespoon capers
    1/4 red onion, thinly sliced
    Fresh dill sprigs, for garnish
    Lemon wedges, for serving

Instructions:

    Prepare the Bagel:
- Slice the bagel in half.

    Spread Cream Cheese:
- Spread a generous layer of softened cream cheese on each half of the bagel.

    Add Smoked Salmon:
- Lay the smoked salmon (lox) over the cream cheese on each bagel half.

    Top with Toppings:
- Sprinkle capers over the smoked salmon. Add thinly sliced red onion on top.

    Garnish with Fresh Dill:
- Garnish the bagel with fresh dill sprigs for added flavor and presentation.

    Serve with Lemon Wedges:
- Serve the bagel with lox and cream cheese with lemon wedges on the side for squeezing over the top.

    Enjoy:
- Enjoy your classic and delicious Bagel with Lox and Cream Cheese!

This classic combination is a popular choice for breakfast or brunch and is known for its rich and satisfying flavors. The creaminess of the cheese, the smokiness of the salmon, and the brininess of the capers come together for a delightful and savory experience.

Sun-Dried Tomato and Basil Egg Muffins

Ingredients:

6 large eggs
1/4 cup milk
1/4 cup sun-dried tomatoes, chopped
2 tablespoons fresh basil, chopped
1/4 cup feta cheese, crumbled
Salt and black pepper to taste
Cooking spray or olive oil for greasing the muffin tin

Instructions:

Preheat the Oven:
- Preheat your oven to 375°F (190°C).

Prepare Muffin Tin:
- Grease a 6-cup muffin tin with cooking spray or a light coating of olive oil.

Whisk Eggs:
- In a bowl, whisk together the eggs and milk until well combined.

Add Ingredients:
- Stir in the chopped sun-dried tomatoes, fresh basil, and crumbled feta cheese into the egg mixture.

Season:
- Season the mixture with salt and black pepper to taste. Remember that feta cheese can be salty, so adjust accordingly.

Pour into Muffin Cups:
- Pour the egg mixture evenly into the prepared muffin cups.

Bake:
- Bake in the preheated oven for 15-20 minutes or until the egg muffins are set in the center.

Cool and Serve:
- Allow the egg muffins to cool slightly before removing them from the muffin tin.

Serve Warm or Refrigerate:
- Serve the Sun-Dried Tomato and Basil Egg Muffins warm. They can also be refrigerated for later use.

Optional:

- Variations: Feel free to add other ingredients such as spinach, bell peppers, or mushrooms for additional flavor and nutrients.
- Make-Ahead: These egg muffins can be made ahead of time and stored in the refrigerator. Reheat in the microwave or oven before serving.

These Sun-Dried Tomato and Basil Egg Muffins are a convenient and tasty breakfast option. Packed with Mediterranean flavors, they are not only delicious but also versatile and easy to customize based on your preferences.

Blueberry Lemon Poppy Seed Pancakes

Ingredients:

    1 cup all-purpose flour
    2 tablespoons granulated sugar
    1 teaspoon baking powder
    1/2 teaspoon baking soda
    1/4 teaspoon salt
    1 tablespoon poppy seeds
    Zest of 1 lemon
    1 cup buttermilk
    1 large egg
    2 tablespoons unsalted butter, melted
    1 cup fresh blueberries
    Butter or cooking spray for greasing the griddle
    Maple syrup for serving

Instructions:

    Preheat Griddle:
- Preheat a griddle or non-stick pan over medium heat.

    Mix Dry Ingredients:
- In a bowl, whisk together the flour, sugar, baking powder, baking soda, salt, poppy seeds, and lemon zest.

    Combine Wet Ingredients:
- In another bowl, whisk together the buttermilk, egg, and melted butter.

    Create Batter:
- Pour the wet ingredients into the dry ingredients and stir until just combined. It's okay if the batter has some lumps.

    Fold in Blueberries:
- Gently fold in the fresh blueberries into the batter.

    Grease Griddle:
- Grease the griddle with butter or cooking spray.

    Pour Batter:
- Pour 1/4 cup portions of batter onto the griddle for each pancake. Use the back of a spoon to spread the batter into a round shape.

    Cook Until Bubbles Form:

- Cook until bubbles form on the surface of the pancakes and the edges start to look set.

Flip and Cook Other Side:
- Carefully flip the pancakes and cook the other side until golden brown.

Repeat:
- Repeat the process with the remaining batter, adding more butter or cooking spray to the griddle as needed.

Keep Warm:
- Keep the cooked pancakes warm in a low oven until ready to serve.

Serve with Maple Syrup:
- Serve the Blueberry Lemon Poppy Seed Pancakes warm, drizzled with maple syrup.

Enjoy:
- Enjoy these flavorful and fluffy pancakes that combine the sweetness of blueberries with the citrusy brightness of lemon and the crunch of poppy seeds.

These Blueberry Lemon Poppy Seed Pancakes are a delightful twist on traditional pancakes, offering a burst of fruity and zesty flavors in every bite. Perfect for a delicious breakfast or brunch treat!

Avocado and Bacon Breakfast Sandwich

Ingredients:

2 slices of your favorite bread (such as ciabatta or whole grain)
2 large eggs
2 slices of cooked bacon
1/2 ripe avocado, sliced
Salt and black pepper to taste
Butter or cooking spray for the eggs
Optional: Hot sauce or sriracha for added spice
Optional: Sliced tomatoes or lettuce for extra freshness

Instructions:

Cook Bacon:
- Cook the bacon slices until crispy. Drain excess grease on a paper towel.

Toast the Bread:
- Toast the slices of bread to your liking.

Prepare Avocado:
- Slice the ripe avocado and season with a pinch of salt and black pepper.

Cook Eggs:
- In a skillet, melt a small amount of butter or use cooking spray. Fry the eggs to your desired level of doneness (fried or scrambled).

Assemble the Sandwich:
- Place one slice of toasted bread on a plate.

Layer Ingredients:
- On the bread, layer the cooked bacon, sliced avocado, and cooked eggs. If desired, add hot sauce or sriracha for a spicy kick.

Optional Fresh Ingredients:
- Add sliced tomatoes or lettuce for extra freshness if you like.

Top with Second Slice:
- Place the second slice of toasted bread on top to complete the sandwich.

Serve Immediately:
- Serve the Avocado and Bacon Breakfast Sandwich immediately while the ingredients are warm.

Enjoy:

- Enjoy this delicious and satisfying breakfast sandwich that combines the creaminess of avocado with the savory goodness of bacon and eggs.

Feel free to customize this sandwich based on your preferences. You can experiment with different types of bread, add cheese, or include other favorite toppings to make it your own.

Pesto and Sundried Tomato Frittata

Ingredients:

    6 large eggs
    1/4 cup milk
    Salt and black pepper to taste
    2 tablespoons pesto sauce
    1/4 cup sun-dried tomatoes, chopped
    1/2 cup shredded mozzarella cheese
    2 tablespoons grated Parmesan cheese
    1 tablespoon olive oil
    Fresh basil leaves for garnish (optional)

Instructions:

Preheat Oven:
- Preheat your oven broiler.

Whisk Eggs:
- In a bowl, whisk together the eggs, milk, salt, and black pepper until well combined.

Add Pesto and Tomatoes:
- Stir in the pesto sauce and chopped sun-dried tomatoes into the egg mixture.

Prep Cheeses:
- Mix the shredded mozzarella and grated Parmesan cheeses together in a small bowl.

Heat Olive Oil:
- Heat olive oil in an oven-safe skillet over medium heat.

Pour Egg Mixture:
- Pour the egg mixture into the skillet, distributing it evenly.

Sprinkle Cheeses:
- Sprinkle the mixed cheeses over the top of the eggs.

Cook on Stovetop:
- Cook on the stovetop without stirring for 3-4 minutes until the edges begin to set.

Broil in Oven:

- Transfer the skillet to the preheated oven broiler and broil for an additional 3-5 minutes until the top is set and golden brown.

Check Doneness:
- Ensure the center is cooked by gently shaking the pan; it should be set but slightly jiggly.

Garnish and Serve:
- Garnish with fresh basil leaves if desired.

Serve Warm:
- Allow the frittata to cool for a few minutes before slicing. Serve warm.

Enjoy:
- Enjoy this flavorful Pesto and Sundried Tomato Frittata as a delicious and satisfying breakfast or brunch option.

Feel free to customize this frittata by adding other ingredients such as sautéed vegetables or different types of cheese to suit your taste preferences.

Chocolate Banana Bread

Ingredients:

    3 ripe bananas, mashed
    1/2 cup unsalted butter, melted
    1 teaspoon vanilla extract
    2 large eggs
    1 cup granulated sugar
    1 1/2 cups all-purpose flour
    1/2 cup unsweetened cocoa powder
    1 teaspoon baking soda
    1/4 teaspoon salt
    1/2 cup sour cream or plain Greek yogurt
    1 cup chocolate chips (semi-sweet or dark), divided
    Optional: Chopped nuts (such as walnuts or pecans)

Instructions:

Preheat Oven:
- Preheat your oven to 350°F (175°C). Grease and flour a 9x5-inch loaf pan.

Mash Bananas:
- In a bowl, mash the ripe bananas with a fork until smooth.

Combine Wet Ingredients:
- In a large mixing bowl, combine the melted butter, mashed bananas, vanilla extract, eggs, and granulated sugar. Mix until well combined.

Sift Dry Ingredients:
- In a separate bowl, sift together the flour, cocoa powder, baking soda, and salt.

Add Dry Ingredients to Wet Ingredients:
- Gradually add the sifted dry ingredients to the wet ingredients, stirring until just combined.

Add Sour Cream or Yogurt:
- Fold in the sour cream or plain Greek yogurt until the batter is smooth.

Fold in Chocolate Chips:
- Gently fold in 3/4 cup of chocolate chips into the batter. Reserve the remaining chocolate chips for topping.

Optional: Add Nuts:

- If desired, add chopped nuts to the batter.

Pour into Loaf Pan:
- Pour the batter into the prepared loaf pan, spreading it evenly.

Top with Chocolate Chips:
- Sprinkle the remaining 1/4 cup of chocolate chips on top of the batter.

Bake:
- Bake in the preheated oven for 60-70 minutes or until a toothpick inserted into the center comes out clean or with a few moist crumbs.

Cool:
- Allow the chocolate banana bread to cool in the pan for about 15 minutes, then transfer it to a wire rack to cool completely.

Slice and Enjoy:
- Once cooled, slice and enjoy the rich and moist Chocolate Banana Bread!

This chocolate-infused banana bread is a delightful treat for chocolate lovers. The combination of ripe bananas and cocoa creates a moist and flavorful bread that's perfect for breakfast, snack, or dessert.

Cheesy Spinach and Artichoke Breakfast Casserole

Ingredients:

    8 large eggs
    1 cup milk
    1 cup shredded cheddar cheese
    1 cup shredded mozzarella cheese
    1/2 cup grated Parmesan cheese
    1 (10-ounce) package frozen chopped spinach, thawed and drained
    1 (14-ounce) can artichoke hearts, drained and chopped
    1/2 cup mayonnaise
    1 teaspoon garlic powder
    1/2 teaspoon onion powder
    Salt and black pepper to taste
    Cooking spray for greasing the baking dish

Instructions:

Preheat Oven:
- Preheat your oven to 375°F (190°C).

Prepare Baking Dish:
- Grease a 9x13-inch baking dish with cooking spray.

Mix Eggs and Milk:
- In a large bowl, whisk together the eggs and milk until well combined.

Add Cheeses:
- Add the shredded cheddar, shredded mozzarella, and grated Parmesan cheese to the egg mixture. Stir to combine.

Add Spinach and Artichokes:
- Add the thawed and drained chopped spinach, as well as the chopped artichoke hearts, to the bowl. Mix well.

Incorporate Mayo and Seasonings:
- Stir in the mayonnaise, garlic powder, onion powder, salt, and black pepper until all ingredients are evenly incorporated.

Pour into Baking Dish:
- Pour the mixture into the prepared baking dish, spreading it evenly.

Bake:

- Bake in the preheated oven for 25-30 minutes or until the casserole is set and the top is golden brown.

Cool Slightly:
- Allow the casserole to cool slightly before slicing.

Slice and Serve:
- Slice into squares or rectangles and serve warm.

Garnish (Optional):
- Garnish with additional grated Parmesan cheese, chopped fresh herbs, or a dollop of sour cream if desired.

Enjoy:
- Enjoy this Cheesy Spinach and Artichoke Breakfast Casserole as a delicious and savory breakfast or brunch option.

This flavorful breakfast casserole combines the classic spinach and artichoke dip flavors with the heartiness of eggs and cheese. It's a great make-ahead dish for feeding a crowd or for a leisurely weekend brunch.

Vanilla Berry Parfait with Granola

Ingredients:

    2 cups mixed berries (strawberries, blueberries, raspberries)
    2 cups vanilla yogurt
    1 cup granola
    Honey for drizzling (optional)
    Fresh mint leaves for garnish (optional)

Instructions:

    Prepare Berries:
- Wash and hull the strawberries, then slice them into bite-sized pieces if desired.

    Layering the Parfait:
- Begin by adding a spoonful of vanilla yogurt to the bottom of each parfait glass or bowl.

    Add Berries:
- Add a layer of mixed berries on top of the yogurt.

    Sprinkle Granola:
- Sprinkle a layer of granola over the berries. This adds a crunchy texture to the parfait.

    Repeat Layers:
- Repeat the layering process by adding more vanilla yogurt, berries, and granola until the glass or bowl is filled.

    Drizzle with Honey (Optional):
- If desired, drizzle honey over the top for added sweetness.

    Garnish with Mint (Optional):
- Garnish with fresh mint leaves for a burst of freshness.

    Serve Immediately:
- Serve the Vanilla Berry Parfait with Granola immediately and enjoy the delightful combination of creamy yogurt, sweet berries, and crunchy granola.

This Vanilla Berry Parfait with Granola is a refreshing and wholesome dessert or breakfast option. It's not only visually appealing but also packed with the goodness of fresh berries and the crunch of granola. Feel free to customize it with your favorite fruits or nuts for added variety.

Ham and Swiss Croissant Sandwiches

Ingredients:

- 4 large croissants
- 8 slices of ham
- 4 slices Swiss cheese
- Dijon mustard
- Mayonnaise
- Butter for toasting (optional)
- Lettuce leaves (optional)
- Tomato slices (optional)

Instructions:

Preheat Oven (Optional):
- Preheat your oven to 350°F (175°C) if you prefer warm sandwiches.

Slice Croissants:
- Slice the croissants in half horizontally, creating a top and bottom for each sandwich.

Spread Condiments:
- On the bottom half of each croissant, spread a layer of Dijon mustard and mayonnaise according to your taste.

Layer Ham:
- Place two slices of ham on each bottom half of the croissants.

Add Swiss Cheese:
- Top the ham with a slice of Swiss cheese.

Optional Additions:
- If desired, add lettuce leaves and tomato slices on top of the Swiss cheese.

Assemble Sandwiches:
- Place the top half of each croissant over the filling, creating a sandwich.

Optional Toasting (Optional):
- For a warm and slightly toasted sandwich, melt a small amount of butter in a skillet and toast the assembled croissants on both sides until the cheese is melted.

Serve Warm or Cold:

- Serve the Ham and Swiss Croissant Sandwiches warm or at room temperature.

Enjoy:
- Enjoy these delicious and savory croissant sandwiches with your favorite sides.

These Ham and Swiss Croissant Sandwiches are a classic and delightful choice for breakfast, brunch, or lunch. The combination of tender ham, melted Swiss cheese, and flaky croissants creates a satisfying and flavorful meal. Feel free to customize the sandwiches with additional toppings or condiments to suit your preferences.

Sourdough Breakfast Strata with Ham and Gruyere

Ingredients:

8 cups sourdough bread, cut into cubes
1 1/2 cups cooked ham, diced
1 1/2 cups Gruyere cheese, shredded
1/2 cup Parmesan cheese, grated
1/2 cup green onions, finely chopped
8 large eggs
2 1/2 cups milk
1/4 cup unsalted butter, melted
1 tablespoon Dijon mustard
1 teaspoon dried thyme
Salt and black pepper to taste
Cooking spray or extra butter for greasing the baking dish

Instructions:

Preheat Oven:
- Preheat your oven to 350°F (175°C).

Prepare Baking Dish:
- Grease a 9x13-inch baking dish with cooking spray or butter.

Layer Bread, Ham, and Cheese:
- In the prepared baking dish, layer half of the sourdough cubes, followed by half of the diced ham, half of the shredded Gruyere, and half of the grated Parmesan. Repeat with the remaining sourdough, ham, Gruyere, and Parmesan.

Whisk Eggs and Milk:
- In a large bowl, whisk together the eggs, milk, melted butter, Dijon mustard, dried thyme, salt, and black pepper until well combined.

Pour Egg Mixture:
- Pour the egg mixture evenly over the layered bread, ham, and cheese in the baking dish.

Press Down:
- Gently press down on the bread mixture with a spatula to ensure it's evenly soaked in the egg mixture.

Add Green Onions:

- Sprinkle the finely chopped green onions over the top.

Cover and Refrigerate (Optional):
- At this point, you can cover the baking dish with plastic wrap and refrigerate it overnight for the flavors to meld.

Bake:
- Bake in the preheated oven for 45-50 minutes or until the strata is set and the top is golden brown.

Cool Slightly:
- Allow the Sourdough Breakfast Strata to cool for a few minutes before slicing.

Slice and Serve:
- Slice into squares or rectangles and serve warm.

Enjoy:
- Enjoy this flavorful and satisfying Sourdough Breakfast Strata with Ham and Gruyere for a delicious brunch or breakfast.

This make-ahead breakfast strata is perfect for entertaining guests or for a hearty family brunch. The combination of sourdough, ham, Gruyere, and aromatic herbs creates a savory and comforting dish that's sure to be a hit.

Coconut Pineapple Smoothie Bowl

Ingredients:

For the Smoothie Bowl:

    1 cup frozen pineapple chunks
    1/2 banana, frozen
    1/2 cup coconut milk
    1/4 cup Greek yogurt
    1 tablespoon honey or maple syrup (optional, for sweetness)

For Toppings:

    Fresh pineapple chunks
    Shredded coconut
    Granola
    Chia seeds
    Sliced strawberries or other berries

Instructions:

    Prepare Smoothie Base:
- In a blender, combine the frozen pineapple chunks, frozen banana, coconut milk, Greek yogurt, and honey or maple syrup (if using).

    Blend Until Smooth:
- Blend the ingredients until smooth and creamy. If the mixture is too thick, you can add a bit more coconut milk to reach your desired consistency.

    Pour into a Bowl:
- Pour the smoothie into a bowl.

    Add Toppings:
- Arrange fresh pineapple chunks, shredded coconut, granola, chia seeds, and sliced strawberries or other berries on top of the smoothie.

    Optional Garnish:
- Optionally, you can sprinkle additional shredded coconut or drizzle honey over the top for added sweetness.

    Serve Immediately:

- Serve the Coconut Pineapple Smoothie Bowl immediately.

Enjoy:
- Enjoy this refreshing and tropical smoothie bowl as a nutritious breakfast or a satisfying snack.

This Coconut Pineapple Smoothie Bowl is not only delicious but also packed with tropical flavors and nutrients. The combination of pineapple, coconut, and other wholesome ingredients creates a delightful and visually appealing breakfast or snack. Customize the toppings based on your preferences for a personalized treat.

Almond Joy Overnight Oats

Ingredients:

1/2 cup rolled oats
1/2 cup almond milk (or any milk of your choice)
1 tablespoon chia seeds
1 tablespoon unsweetened shredded coconut
1 tablespoon cocoa powder
1-2 tablespoons maple syrup or sweetener of choice (adjust to taste)
1/4 teaspoon almond extract
1 tablespoon chopped almonds
1 tablespoon mini chocolate chips
Optional: Sliced bananas or additional shredded coconut for topping

Instructions:

Mix Dry Ingredients:
- In a jar or airtight container, combine the rolled oats, chia seeds, shredded coconut, cocoa powder, chopped almonds, and mini chocolate chips.

Add Wet Ingredients:
- Pour in the almond milk and add the almond extract and maple syrup.

Stir Well:
- Stir the ingredients well until everything is evenly combined.

Refrigerate Overnight:
- Cover the jar or container and refrigerate the mixture overnight or for at least 4-6 hours.

Stir Before Serving:
- Before serving, give the overnight oats a good stir to make sure everything is well-mixed.

Add Toppings:
- Top the oats with sliced bananas, additional shredded coconut, or any other toppings of your choice.

Enjoy:
- Enjoy the Almond Joy Overnight Oats straight from the fridge for a quick and delicious breakfast.

These Almond Joy Overnight Oats are a tasty and convenient way to enjoy the flavors of the classic candy bar in a nutritious breakfast. The combination of oats, almond milk, coconut, and chocolate creates a delightful and satisfying meal that can be prepared ahead of time. Feel free to adjust the sweetness and toppings to suit your taste preferences.

Breakfast Tiramisu French Toast

Ingredients:

For the French Toast:

    4 slices of thick bread (challah or brioche works well)
    3 large eggs
    1/2 cup whole milk
    1 teaspoon instant coffee granules dissolved in 1 tablespoon hot water
    2 tablespoons unsweetened cocoa powder
    1 teaspoon vanilla extract
    Pinch of salt
    Butter for cooking

For the Tiramisu Topping:

    1 cup mascarpone cheese
    1/4 cup powdered sugar
    1 teaspoon cocoa powder (for dusting)
    1 shot of espresso or 1/4 cup strong brewed coffee, cooled
    Chocolate shavings (optional, for garnish)

Instructions:

    Prepare French Toast Mixture:
- In a bowl, whisk together eggs, milk, dissolved coffee, cocoa powder, vanilla extract, and a pinch of salt.

    Dip Bread Slices:
- Dip each slice of bread into the egg mixture, ensuring both sides are well-coated.

    Cook French Toast:
- In a skillet over medium heat, melt butter. Cook the dipped bread slices until golden brown on both sides.

    Prepare Tiramisu Topping:
- In a separate bowl, whisk together mascarpone cheese and powdered sugar until smooth.

    Layer French Toast:

- Once the French toast slices are cooked, spread a generous layer of the mascarpone mixture between the slices, creating a layered effect.

Drizzle Espresso or Coffee:
- Drizzle a shot of espresso or 1/4 cup of strong brewed coffee over the layered French toast.

Dust with Cocoa Powder:
- Dust the top of the French toast with cocoa powder.

Optional Garnish:
- Optionally, garnish with chocolate shavings for added elegance.

Serve Immediately:
- Serve the Breakfast Tiramisu French Toast immediately while it's warm.

Enjoy:
- Enjoy this delightful and indulgent breakfast that combines the flavors of classic Tiramisu with the comforting appeal of French toast.

This Breakfast Tiramisu French Toast is a luxurious twist on a classic breakfast dish. The combination of coffee-infused French toast, creamy mascarpone, and cocoa creates a delightful and indulgent morning treat that will make you feel like you're enjoying dessert for breakfast.

www.ingramcontent.com/pod-product-compliance
Lightning Source LLC
LaVergne TN
LVHW061940070526
838199LV00060B/3894